LOVE

D1337362

Robert Atwell is an Anglican priest. After six years as Chaplain of Trinity College, Cambridge, he became a Benedictine monk, spending the next ten years in a monastery in the Cotswolds.

He is the compiler of two volumes of daily readings for the liturgical year, *Celebrating the Saints* and *Celebrating the Seasons,* both published by the Canterbury Press.

He is presently vicar of the parish of St Mary the Virgin, Primrose Hill, in London.

MORAY COUNCIL LIBRARIES & INFO.SERVICES	
20 15 75 50	
Askews	
808.803543	

LOVE

100 readings
in celebration of
marriage and love

compiled by
Robert Atwell

CANTERBURY
PRESS
Norwich

© in this compilation Robert Atwell 2005

First published in 2005 by the Canterbury Press Norwich
(a publishing imprint of Hymns Ancient & Modern Limited,
a registered charity)
9–17 St Albans Place, London N1 0NX

www.scm-canterburypress.co.uk

All rights reserved. No part of this publication may be
reproduced, stored in a retrieval system, or transmitted,
in any form or by any means, electronic, mechanical,
photocopying or otherwise, without the prior permission
of the publisher, Canterbury Press

British Library Cataloguing in Publication data

A catalogue record for this book is available
from the British Library

ISBN 1-85311-600-9

Typeset by Regent Typesetting, London
Printed and bound by
Creative Print and Design

Contents

Introduction

Weddings are great events not simply for the couple getting married, but for their families and friends, and indeed the entire local community. Weddings bring people together in friendship and celebration. They are occasions full of promise and joy, as two young people declare their love for one another and their intention to share the rest of their lives together. Weddings can be fun too – provided the photographs don't go on for ever.

Equally memorable are significant anniversaries, particularly a couple's silver or golden wedding. You suddenly realize how the years have flown past, and how the relationship has changed and matured. Their knowledge and understanding of each another have deepened. They will have doubtless been through bad times as well as good, but somehow they have stuck together, and in the process learned to forgive one another when mistakes have been made or if trust has been breached. Such anniversaries are always special because at the most profound level they are a celebration of human friendship. They are opportunities for thanksgiving not simply for love, but of loyalty and for the stability they have created for others.

'Love and marriage go together like a horse and carriage,' as the old song has it. Except, of course, they don't always. When love and marriage do go hand-in-hand it is indeed wonderful. But we all know of loveless marriages that have gone sour and broken down, where love has been supplanted by conflict. We also know of couples and individuals who are unable to express their love through marriage. Failure and the sheer complexity of our lives point up the danger of being sentimental when it comes to talk about relationships. We need to be both realistic as well as idealistic in what we say.

This anthology of readings explores both the real and the ideal in relation to love, marriage, and friendship across the centuries. It is not a comprehensive selection. Nevertheless, it does contain a wide range of material. There are songs, psalms and poems, readings from the Bible, the reflections of various ancient and contemporary writers, with a bit of humour thrown in for good measure. The readings can stand alone and be used at weddings, engagement parties, the renewal of vows, and family celebrations, or be used privately for personal reflection. Collectively, they form a tapestry of wisdom not only about the joy of love, but also the struggle to love. Above all, they remind us just what a precious gift the love and commitment of another human being is, and what a privilege it is when you have someone to 'have and to hold' till death you do part.

Robert Atwell

To love and to cherish

It was a lover and his lass

It was a lover and his lass,
   With a hey, and a ho, and hey nonino,
That o'er the green corn-field did pass,
   In spring time, the only pretty ring time,
When birds do sing, hey ding a ding, ding;
   Sweet lovers love the spring.

Between the acres of the rye,
   With a hey, and a ho, and a hey nonino,
Those pretty country folks would lie,
   In spring time, the only pretty ring time,
When birds do sing, hey ding a ding, ding;
   Sweet lovers love the spring.

This carol they began that hour,
   With a hey, and a ho, and hey nonino,
How that a life was but a flower
   In spring time, the only pretty ring time,
When birds do sing, hey ding a ding, ding;
   Sweet lovers love the spring.

And therefore take the present time,
   With a hey, and a ho, and hey nonino,
For love is crowned with the prime
   In spring time, the only pretty ring time,
When birds do sing, hey ding a ding, ding;
   Sweet lovers love the spring.

William Shakespeare (1564–1616), *Songs Sung in Arden*

Time of roses

It was not in the winter
  Our loving lot was cast;
It was the time of roses –
  We pluck'd them as we pass'd!
That churlish season never frown'd
  On early lovers yet:
O no – the world was newly crown'd
  With flowers when first we met!
'Twas twilight, and I bade you go,
  But still you held me fast;
It was the time of roses –
  We pluck'd them as we pass'd!

Thomas Hood (1799–1845)

Set me as a seal upon your heart

My beloved speaks and says to me:
  'Arise, my love, my fair one,
    and come away;
    for now the winter is past,
    the rain is over and gone.
The flowers appear on the earth again;
    the time of singing has come,
    and the voice of the turtle dove
    is once again heard in our land.
  The fig tree puts forth its figs,
    and the vines are in blossom;

they give forth their fragrance.
Arise my love, my fair one,
and come away.'

Set me as a seal upon your heart,
as a seal upon your arm:
for love is strong as death,
passion as cruel as the grave:
its flashes are flashes of fire,
a raging flame.
Many waters cannot quench love,
neither can the floods drown it.
If one offered for love
all the wealth of one's house,
it would be utterly scorned.
For love is as strong as death.

The Song of Songs, the Bible

Song to Celia

Drink to me, only with thine eyes,
     And I will pledge with mine;
Or leave a kiss but in the cup,
     And I'll not look for wine.
The thirst, that from the soul doth rise,
     Doth ask a drink divine:
But might I of Jove's nectar sup,
     I would not change for thine.
I sent thee, late, a rosie wreath,

Not so much honouring thee,
As giving it a hope, that there
It could not withered be.
But thou thereon did'st only breathe,
And sent'st it back to me:
Since when it grows, and smells, I swear,
Not of itself, but thee.

Ben Jonson (1573?–1637)

O Mistress mine, where are you roaming?

O Mistress mine, where are you roaming?
O stay and hear; your true-love's coming,
That can sing both high and low.
Trip no further, pretty sweeting;
Journeys end in lovers meeting.
Every wise man's son doth know.

What is love? 'Tis not hereafter;
Present mirth hath present laughter;
What's to come is still unsure;
In delay there lies no plenty;
Then come kiss me, sweet and twenty!
Youth's a stuff will not endure.

William Shakespeare (1564–1616), 'Song', *Twelfth Night*

[6]

Come into the garden, Maud

Come into the garden, Maud,
  For the black bat, night, has flown,
Come into the garden, Maud
  I am here at the gate alone;
And the woodbine spices are wafted abroad,
  And the musk of the rose is blown.

For a breeze of morning moves,
  And the planet of Love is on high,
Beginning to faint in the light that she loves
  On a bed of daffodil sky,
To faint in the light of the sun she loves,
  To faint in his light, and to die.

Alfred, Lord Tennyson (1809–92), *Maud*

Flapper

Love has crept out of her sealèd heart
  As a field-bee, black and amber,
Breaks from the winter-cell, to clamber
Up the warm grass where the sunbeams start.

Mischief has come in her dawning eyes,
And a glint of coloured iris brings
Such as lies along the folded wings
Of the bee before he flies.

Who, with a ruffling, careful breath,
Has opened the wings of the wild young sprite?
Has fluttered her spirit to stumbling flight
In her eyes, as a young bee stumbleth?

Love makes the burden of her voice.
The hum of his heavy, staggering wings
Sets quivering with wisdom the common things
That she says, and her words rejoice.

D. H. Lawrence (1885–1930)

Come live with me and be my love

Come live with me and be my love,
    And we will all the pleasures prove
That hills and valleys, dale and field,
And all the craggy mountains yield.

And we will sit upon the rocks,
And see the shepherds feed their flocks,
By shallow rivers to whose falls
Melodious birds sing madrigals.

There will I make thee beds of roses
And a thousand fragrant posies,
A cap of flowers, and a kirtle
Embroidered all with leaves of myrtle.

A gown made of the finest wool,
Which from our pretty lambs we pull,
Fair lined slippers for the cold,
With buckles of the purest gold.

The shepherds' swains shall dance and sing
For thy delight each May-morning:
If these delights thy mind may move,
Then live with me and be my love.

Christopher Marlowe (1564–93), *The Passionate Shepherd
to his Love*

Jeanie with the light brown hair

I dream of Jeanie with the light brown hair,
　Borne, like a vapour, on the summer air;
I see her tripping where the bright streams play,
Happy as the daisies that dance on her way.
Many were the wild notes her merry voice would pour,
Many were the blithe birds that warbled them o'er:
Oh! I dream of Jeanie with the light brown hair,
Floating, like a vapour, on the soft summer air.

I sigh for Jeanie, but her light form strayed
Far from the fond hearts 'round her native glade;
Her smiles have vanished and her sweet songs flown,
Flitting like the dream that have cheered us and gone.
Now the nodding wild flowers may wither on the shore
While her gentle fingers will cull them no more:
Oh! I sigh for Jeanie with the light brown hair,
Floating, like a vapour, on the soft summer air.

Stephen Foster (1826–64)

But, soft! what light through yonder window breaks?

But, soft! what light through yonder window breaks?
It is the east, and Juliet is the sun.
Arise, fair sun, and kill the envious moon,
Who is already sick and pale with grief
That thou her maid art far more fair than she.
Be not her maid, since she is envious;
Her vestal livery is but sick and green,
And none but fools do wear it; cast it off.
It is my lady: O, it is my love!
O, that she knew she were!
She speaks, yet she says nothing: what of that?
Her eye discourses; I will answer it.
I am too bold, 'tis not to me she speaks;
Two of the fairest stars in all the heaven,
Having some business, do entreat her eyes
To twinkle in their spheres till they return . . . .
See, how she leans her cheek upon her hand!
O that I were a glove upon that hand,
That I might touch that cheek!

William Shakespeare (1564–1616), *Romeo and Juliet*

O Romeo, Romeo! wherefore art thou Romeo?

O Romeo, Romeo! wherefore art thou Romeo?
  Deny thy father and refuse thy name;
Or, if thou wilt not, be but sworn my love,
And I'll no longer be a Capulet . . .

'Tis but thy name that is my enemy;
Thou art thyself, though not a Montague.
What's Montague? It is nor hand nor foot,
Nor arm, nor face, nor any other part
Belonging to a man. O, be some other name!
What's in a name? that which we call a rose
By any other name would smell as sweet;
So Romeo would, were he not Romeo call'd,
Retain that dear perfection which he owes
Without that title. Romeo, doff thy name;
And for thy name, which is no part of thee,
Take all myself.

William Shakespeare (1564–1616), *Romeo and Juliet*

The Sun rising

Busie old fool, unruly Sun,
　　Why dost thou thus,
Through windows, and through curtains call on us?
Must to thy motions lovers' seasons run?
　　Saucy pedantic wretch, go chide
　　Late school-boys, and sour 'prentices,
Go tell court huntsmen, that the King will ride,
Call country ants to harvest offices;
Love, all alike, no season knows, no clime,
Nor hours, days, months, which are the rags of time.

　　Thy beams, so reverend, and strong
　　Why shouldst thou think?
I could eclipse and cloud them with a wink,
But that I would not lose her sight so long:
　　If her eyes have not blinded thine,
　　Look, and tomorrow late, tell me,
Whether both the Indias of spice and mine
Be where thou left'st them, or lie here with me.
Ask for those kings whom thou saw'st yesterday,
And thou shalt hear, 'All here in one bed lay.'

　　She's all States, and all Princes I;
　　Nothing else is.
Princes do but play us; compared to this,
All honour's mimic; all wealth alchemy.
　　Thou, Sun, art half as happy as we,
　　In that the world's contracted thus;
Thine age asks ease, and since thy duties be

To warm the world, that's done in warming us.
Shine here to us, and thou art everywhere;
This bed thy centre is, these walls thy sphere.

John Donne (1572–1631)

To his coy mistress

Had we but world enough, and time,
This coyness, Lady, were no crime.
We would sit down and think which way
To walk and pass our long love's day.
Thou by the Indian Ganges' side
Should'st rubies find: I by the tide
Of Humber would complain. I would
Love you ten years before the flood,
And you should, if you please, refuse
Till the conversion of the Jews.
My vegetable love should grow
Vaster than empires, and more slow.
An hundred years should go to praise
Thine eyes and on thy forehead gaze;
Two hundred to adore each breast,
But thirty thousand to the rest.
An age at least to every part,
And the last age should show your heart.
For, Lady, you deserve this state,
Nor would I love at lower rate.
      But at my back I always hear
Time's wingèd chariot hurrying near;

And yonder all before us lie
Deserts of vast eternity.
Thy beauty shall no more be found,
Nor in my marble vault, shall sound
My echoing song: then worms shall try
That long preserved virginity,
And your quaint honour turn to dust,
And into ashes all my lust.
The grave's a fine and private place,
But none, I think, do there embrace.
      Now therefore, while the youthful hue
Sits on thy skin like morning dew,
And while thy willing soul transpires
At every pore with instant fires,
Now let us sport us while we may,
And now, like amorous birds of prey,
Rather at once our time devour
Than languish in his slow-chapt power.
Let us roll all our strength and all
Our sweetness up into one ball,
And tear our pleasures with rough strife
Through the iron gates of life:
Thus, though we cannot make our sun
Stand still, yet we will make him run.

Andrew Marvell (1621–78)

He fumbles at your Spirit

He fumbles at your Spirit
    As Players at the Keys
Before they drop full Music on –
He stuns you by degrees –
Prepares your brittle Nature
For the Ethereal Blow
By fainter Hammers – further heard –
Then nearer – Then so slow
Your Breath has time to straighten –
Your Brain – to bubble Cool –
Deals – One – imperial – Thunderbolt –
That scalps your naked Soul –

When Winds take Forests in their Paws
The Universe – is still –

Emily Dickinson (1830–86)

To the virgins, to make much of time

Gather ye rosebuds while ye may,
    Old Time is still a-flying:
And this same flower that smiles today
        Tomorrow will be dying.

The glorious lamp of heaven, the sun,
        The higher he's a-getting,
The sooner will his race be run,
        And nearer he's to setting.

That age is best which is the first,
    When youth and blood are warmer;
But being spent, the worse, and worst
    Times, still succeed the former.

Then be not coy, but use your time:
    And while ye may, go marry;
For having lost but once your prime,
    You may for ever tarry.

Robert Herrick (1591–1674)

The secret

I loved thee, though I told thee not,
    Right early and long,
Thou wert my joy in every spot,
My theme in every song.

And when I saw a stranger face
Where beauty held the claim,
I gave it like a secret grace
The being of thy name.

And all the charms of face or voice
Which I in others see
Are but the recollected choice
Of what I felt for thee.

John Clare (1793–1864)

When in disgrace with fortune and men's eyes

When in disgrace with fortune and men's eyes
    I all alone beweep my outcast state,
And trouble deaf heaven with my bootless cries,
    And look upon myself, and curse my fate,
Wishing me like to one more rich in hope,
    Featured like him, like him with friends possessed,
Desiring this man's art, and that man's scope,
    With what I most enjoy contented least;
Yet in these thoughts myself almost despising,
    Haply I think on thee, and then my state,
Like to the lark at break of day arising
    From sullen earth, sing hymns at heaven's gate;
      For thy sweet love remembered such wealth brings
      That then I scorn to change my state with kings.

William Shakespeare (1564–1616), Sonnet XXIX

That first day

I wish I could remember, that first day,
    First hour, first moment of your meeting me,
    If bright or dim the season, it might be
Summer or Winter for aught I can say;
So unrecorded did it slip away,
    So blind was I to see and to foresee,
    So dull to mark the budding of my tree
That would not blossom yet for many a May.

If only I could recollect it, such
    A day of days! I let it come and go
    As traceless as a thaw of bygone snow;
It seemed to mean so little, meant so much;
If only now I could recall that touch,
    First touch of hand in hand – Did one but know!

Christina Rossetti (1830–94)

First love

I ne'er was struck before that hour
    With love so sudden and so sweet.
Her face it bloomed like a sweet flower
    And stole my heart away complete.
My face turned pale a deadly pale,
    My legs refused to walk away,
And when she looked 'What could I ail?'
    My life and all seemed turned to clay.

And then my blood rushed to my face
    And took my eyesight quite away.
The trees and bushes round the place
    Seemed midnight at noon-day.
I could not see a single thing,
    Words from my eyes did start.
They spoke as chords do from the string,
    And blood burnt round my heart.

Are flowers the winter's choice?
    Is love's bed always snow?

She seemed to hear my silent voice
 Not love's appeals to know.
I never saw so sweet a face
 As that I stood before:
My heart has left its dwelling-place
 And can return no more.

John Clare (1793–1864)

Love's philosophy

The fountains mingle with the river
 And the rivers with the ocean,
The winds of heaven mix for ever
With a sweet emotion;
Nothing in the world is single,
All things by a law divine
In one another's being mingle –
Why not I with thine?

See the mountains kiss high heaven
And the waves clasp one another;
No sister-flower would be forgiven
If it disdain'd its brother:

And the sunlight clasps the earth,
And the moonbeams kiss the sea –
What are all these kissings worth,
If thou kiss not me?

Percy Bysshe Shelley (1792–1822)

Beware, brother, beware

Hey, fellas, yes, you, fellas, listen to me, I got
    something to tell you,
And I want you to listen to every word and govern
    yourselves accordingly.
Now, you see these girls with these fine diamonds,
    fox-furs and fine clothes,
Well, Jack, they're looking for a husband,
And you're listening to a man who knows.
They ain't foolin', and if you fool around with them,
You're gonna get yourself in a schoolin'.

Listen. If she saves you dough, and won't go
    to the show
Beware, Brother, Beware!
If she's easy to kiss and won't resist
Beware, Brother, Beware!
And if you go for a walk, and she listens while you talk
She's tryin' to hook you,
And nobody's lookin' and she asks you to taste
    her cookin'
Don't do it, don't do it!

And if you go to a show and she wants to sit in the
    back row,
Bring her down front, bring her right down front.
If you wanna go for a snack, and she wants to sit in the
    booth in the back
Watch out! She's trying to hook you.

And listen. If she's used to caviar and fine silk
When you go out with her she wanna a hot dog and a
    malted milk
She's trying to get you.
You better listen to me 'cause I'm telling you what's
    being put down.
You better pick up on it.

If she's been used to going to Carnegie Hall
And when you take her to a night-club she wants to
    hear one meat-ball,
If she grabs your hand and says,
'Darling, you're such a nice man,'
Beware!

If her sister calls your brother, you better get further.
I'm telling you, you better watch it.
And if she's acting kind of wild, and she says,
'Darling, give me a trial'
Don't you do it, don't be weak, don't give it to her.
And if she smiles in your face and just melts into place
Let her melt, forget it, let her melt.

(should I tell them no more?)
(tell them everything)

Now listen, if she calls you up on the phone, and says,
'Darling, are you all alone?'
Tell her, you've got three girls with you.
Don't pay no attention to women
Stand up for your rights, be a man.

If you turn out the light and she don't fight
That's the end, it's too late.
She's got you hooked, you might as well stick with her.
(should I tell them no more?)
If you get home about two and don't know what to do
You pull back the curtains, and the whole family's
    looking at you
Get your business straight
Set the date, and don't be late.
Brother, Beware, Beware, Beware!
Brother, you better beware!

Morry Lasco, Dick Adams and Fleecie Moore

If music be the food of love, play on

If music be the food of love, play on,
    Give me excess of it, that, surfeiting,
The appetite may sicken and so die.
That strain again! It had a dying fall;
O! it came o'er my ear like the sweet sound
That breathes upon a bank of violets,
Stealing and giving odour! Enough, no more;
'Tis not so sweet now as it was before.
O spirit of love! How quick and fresh art thou,
That, notwithstanding thy capacity
Receiveth as the sea, nought enters there,
Of what validity and pitch soe'er,
But falls into abatement and low price

Even in a minute. So full of shapes in fancy,
That it alone is high fantastical.

William Shakespeare (1564–1616), *Twelfth Night*

A birthday

My heart is like a singing bird
    Whose nest is in a watered shoot;
My heart is like an apple tree
    Whose boughs are bent with thickset fruit;
My heart is like a rainbow shell
    That paddles in a halcyon sea;
My heart is gladder than all of these
    Because my love is come to me.

Raise me a dais of silk and down;
    Hang it with vair and purple dyes;
Carve it in doves and pomegranates
    And peacocks with a hundred eyes;
Work it in gold and silver grapes,
    In leaves and silver fleurs-de-lys;
Because the birthday of my life
    Is come, my love is come to me.

Christina Rossetti (1830–94)

To my valentine

More than a catbird hates a cat,
  Or a criminal hates a clue,
Or the Axis hates the United States,
That's how much I love you.

I love you more than a duck can swim,
And more than a grapefruit squirts,
I love you more than gin rummy is a bore,
And more than toothache hurts.

As a shipwrecked sailor hates the sea,
Or a juggler hates a shove,
As a hostess detests unexpected guests,
That's how much you I love.

I love you more than a wasp can sting,
And more than the subway jerks,
I love you as much as a beggar needs a crutch,
And more than a hangnail irks.

I swear to you by the stars above,
And below, if such there be,
As the High Court loathes perjurious oaths,
That's how you're loved by me.

Ogden Nash (1902–71)

Valentine Eve

Young girls grow eager as the day retires,
   And smile and whisper round their cottage fires,
Listening for noises in the dusky street,
For tinkling latches and for passing feet,
The prophecies of coming joys to hark,
Of wandering lovers stealing through the dark
Dropping their valentines at beauty's door,
With hearts and darts and love-knots littered o'er.
'Aye' said a gossip by a neighbour's hearth,
While the young girls popped up in tittering mirth
To hear the door creak with heart jumping signs
And footsteps hastening by, and valentines
Drop rustling on the floor.

John Clare (1793–1864)

To love and to remember

To love and to remember; that is good:
   To love and forget; that is not well:
To lapse from love to hatred; that is hell
And death and torment, rightly understood.
Soul dazed by love and sorrow, cheer thy mood;
More blest art thou than mortal tongue can tell:
Ring not thy funeral but thy marriage bell,
And salt with hope thy life's insipid food.
Love is the goal, love is the way we wend,
Love is our parallel unending line

Whose only perfect parallel is Christ,
Beginning not begun, end without end:
For he who hath the heart of God sufficed,
Can satisfy all hearts, – yea, thine and mine.

Christina Rossetti (1830–94)

It is not good for man to be alone

When God created man, in order to establish the good of human society, he said, 'It is not good for the man to be alone: let us make him a helper as his partner.' It was neither from similar nor from the same material that divine might formed this partner, but as a clear inspiration to charity and friendship God produced the woman from the actual substance of the man. How beautiful it is that the second human being should have been taken from the side of the first. In this way nature teaches that human beings are equal and, as it were, collateral. Thus in human affairs there is neither a superior nor an inferior. This is a characteristic of true friendship. From the very beginning nature has implanted this desire for friendship and charity in the human heart, a desire which an inner sense of affection soon increased with a taste of sweetness.

Aelred of Rievaulx (1109–67), *On Spiritual Friendship*

Women, wine, and snuff

Give me women, wine, and snuff
Until I cry out 'hold, enough!'
You may do so sans objection
Till the day of resurrection;
For bless my beard they aye shall be
My beloved Trinity.

John Keats (1795–1821)

Love, first learned in a lady's eyes

But love, first learned in a lady's eyes,
Lives not alone immured in the brain,
But with the motion of all elements
Courses as swift as thought in every power,
And gives to every power a double power,
Above their functions and their offices.
It adds a precious seeing to the eye:
A lover's eyes will gaze an eagle blind.
A lover's ear will hear the lowest sound,
When the suspicious head of theft is stopp'd.
Love's feeling is more soft and sensible
Than are the tender horns of cockled snails:
Love's tongue proves dainty Bacchus gross in taste.
For valour, is not Love a Hercules,
Still climbing trees in the Hesperides?
Subtle as Sphinx; as sweet and musical
As bright Apollo's lute, strung with his hair.

And when Love speaks, the voice of all the gods
Make heaven drowsy with the harmony.
Never durst poet touch a pen to write
Until his ink were temp'red with Love's sighs;
O, then his lines would ravish ears,
And plant in tyrants mild humility.
From women's eyes this doctrine I derive.
They sparkle still the right Promethean fire;
They are the books, the arts, the academes,
That show, contain, and nourish, all the world,
Else none at all in aught proves excellent.
Then fools you were these women to forswear;
Or, keeping what is sworn, you will prove fools.
For wisdom's sake, a word that all men love;
Or for Love's sake, a word that loves all men;
Or for men's sake, the authors of these women;
Or women's sake, by whom we men are men –
Let us once lose ourselves to keep our oaths.
It is religion to be thus forsworn;
For charity itself fulfils the law,
And who can sever love from charity?

William Shakespeare (1564–1616), *Love's Labour's Lost*

Was this the face that launched a thousand ships?

Was this the face that launched a thousand ships?
  And burnt the topless towers of Ilium?
Sweet Helen, make me immortal with a kiss:
Her lips suck forth my soul, see where it flies!
Come Helen, come, give me my soul again.
Here will I dwell, for heaven is in these lips,
And all is dross that is not Helena.
I will be Paris, and for love of thee,
Instead of Troy shall Wertenberg be sack'd;
And I will combat with weak Menelaus,
And wear thy colours on my plumed crest;
Yea, I will wound Achilles in the heel,
And then return to Helen for a kiss.
O thou art fairer than the evening air,
Clad in the beauty of a thousand stars:
Brighter art thou than flaming Jupiter,
When he appear'd to hapless Semele;
More lovely than the monarch of the sky
In wanton Arethusa's azur'd arms;
And none but thou shalt be my paramour.

Christopher Marlowe (1564–93), *Doctor Faustus*

Love is

Love is feeling cold in the back of vans
Love is a fanclub with only two fans
Love is walking holding painstained hands
Love is

Love is fish and chips on winter nights
Love is blankets full of strange delights
Love is when you don't put out the light
Love is

Love is the presents in Christmas shops
Love is when you're feeling Top of the Pops
Love is what happens when the music stops
Love is

Love is white panties lying all forlorn
Love is a pink nightdress still slightly warm
Love is when you have to leave at dawn
Love is

Love is you and love is me
Love is a prison and love is free
Love's what's there when you're away from me
Love is . . .

Adrian Henri (1932–2000)

To have and to hold
from this day forward

Shall I compare thee to a summer's day?

Shall I compare thee to a summer's day?
    Thou art more lovely and more temperate:
Rough winds do shake the darling buds of May,
    And summer's lease hath all too short a date:
Sometime too hot the eye of heaven shines,
    And often is his gold complexion dimmed;
And every fair from fair sometimes declines,
    By chance, or nature's changing course untrimmed;
But thy eternal summer shall not fade,
    Nor lose possession of that fair thou owest,
Nor shall Death brag thou wanderest in his shade,
    When in eternal lines to time thou growest;
        So long as men can breathe, or eyes can see,
        So long lives this, and this gives life to thee.

William Shakespeare (1564–1616), Sonnet XVIII

She walks in beauty

She walks in beauty, like the night
    Of cloudless climes and starry skies;
And all that's best of dark and bright
Meet in her aspect and her eyes:
Thus mellowed to that tender light
Which heaven to gaudy day denies.

One shade the more, one ray the less,
Had half-impair'd the nameless grace

Which waves in every raven tress,
Or softly lightens o'er her face;
Where thoughts serenely sweet express
How pure, how dear their dwelling place.

And on that cheek, and o'er that brow,
So soft, so calm, yet eloquent,
The smiles that win, the tints that glow,
But tell of days in goodness spent,
A mind at peace with all below,
A heart whose love is innocent.

Lord Byron (1788–1824)

To be in want of a wife

It is a truth universally acknowledged, that a single man in possession of a good fortune, must be in want of a wife.

However little known the feeling or views of such a man may be on his first entering a neighbourhood, this truth is so well fixed in the minds of the surrounding families, that he is considered as the rightful property of some one or other of their daughters.

'My dear Mr Bennet,' said his lady to him one day, 'have you heard that Netherfield Park is let at last?'

Mr Bennet replied that he had not.

'But it is,' returned she; 'for Mrs Long has just been here, and she told me all about it.'

Mr Bennet made no answer.

'Do not you want to know who has taken it?' cried his wife impatiently.

'*You* want to tell me, and I have no objection to hearing it.'

This was invitation enough.

'Why, my dear, you must know, Mrs Long says that Netherfield is taken by a young man of large fortune from the north of England; that he came down on Monday in a chaise and four to see the place, and was so much delighted with it that he agreed with Mr Morris immediately; that he is to take possession before Michaelmas; and some of his servants are to be in the house by the end of next week.'

'What is his name?'

'Bingley.'

'Is he married or single?'

'Oh! single, my dear, to be sure! A single man of large fortune; four or five thousand a year. What a fine thing for our girls!'

Jane Austen (1775–1817), *Pride and Prejudice*

Finding a capable wife

A capable wife who can find?
    She is far more precious than jewels.
The heart of her husband trusts in her,
    and he will have no lack of gain.
She does him good, and not harm,
    all the days of her life.

She seeks wool and flax,
       and works with willing hands.
She rises while it is still dark
       and provides food for her household
She considers a field and buys it;
       with the fruit of her hands she plants a vineyard.
She girds herself with strength,
       and makes her arms strong.
She opens her hand to the poor,
       and reaches out her hands to the needy.
She is not afraid for her household when it snows,
       for all her household are clothed in crimson.
She makes herself coverings;
       her clothing is fine linen and purple.
Her husband is known in the city gates,
       taking his seat among the elders of the land.
Strength and dignity are her clothing,
       and she laughs at the time to come.
She opens her mouth with wisdom,
       and the teaching of kindness is on her tongue.
She looks well to the ways of her household,
       and does not eat the bread of idleness.
Her children rise up and call her happy;
       her husband too, and he praises her:
'Many women have done excellently,
       but you surpass them all.'
Charm is deceitful, and beauty is vain,
       but a woman who fears the Lord is to be praised.

Proverbs 31, the Bible

The choice of a wife

First, when it shall please God to bring you to Man's estate, making you capable of that calling, use great providence and circumspection in the choice of your wives, as the root from whence may spring most of your future good or evil:

For it is in the choice of Wife, as in the project of War, wherein to err but once is to be undone for ever. Be informed truly of their inclination, which that there may be a more equal sympathy, compare it with your own, how they agree; for you must know, that every good woman makes not every man a good wife, no otherwise then some good Dish digesteth with every stomach. After that, enquire diligently of her stock and race, from whence she sprung, and how her parents have been affected in their youth.

And as it is the safest walking ever between two extremes, so choose not a wife of such absolute perfection and Beauty, that every carnal eye shall bespeak you injury: neither so base and deformed, that breed contempt in others, and bring you to a loathed bed. Make not choice of a Fool, who will be your daily grief and vexation: for it will irk you so oft as you shall hear her talk and you shall continually find to your sorrow that there is nothing so fulsome as a she-fool.

Banish drunkenness out of your House, and affect him not that is affected thereunto: for it is a vice that impairs health, consumes wealth, and transforms a man into a beast.

Suffer not your Sons to pass the Alps: for they shall exchange for their foreign travel (unless they go better fortified) but other vices for their own virtues, Pride, Blasphemy and Atheism, for Humility, Reverence and Religion.

Go as thou wouldest be met, sit as thou wouldest be found, wear thy apparel in a careless, yet a decent seeming: for affectedness in any thing, is commendable in nothing: and endeavour to be so far from vain-glory, that thou strive in anything rather to be in substance without show, then in show without substance.

Lord Burghley (1520–98), *Lord Burghley's Precepts*

Bei Hennef

The little river twittering in the twilight,
   The wan, wondering look of the pale sky,
This is almost bliss.
And everything shut up and gone to sleep,
All the troubles and anxieties and pain
Gone under the twilight.
Only the twilight now, and the soft 'Sh!' of the river
That will last for ever.
And at last I know my love for you is here;
I can see it all, it is whole like the twilight,
It is large, so large, I could not see it before,
Because of the little lights and flickers and interruptions,
Troubles, anxieties and pains.

You are the call and I am the answer,
You are the wish, and I the fulfilment
You are the night, and I the day.
What else – it is perfect enough.
It is perfectly complete,
You and I,
What more – ?
Strange, how we suffer in spite of this.

D. H. Lawrence (1885–1930)

If thou must love me

If thou must love me, let it be for naught
   Except for love's sake only. Do not say
'I love her for her smile – her look – her way
Of speaking gently, – for a trick of thought
That falls in well with mine, and certes brought
A sense of pleasant ease on such a day' –
For these things in themselves, Beloved, may
Be changed, or change for thee – and love, so wrought,
May be unwrought so. Neither love me for
Thine own dear pity's wiping my cheeks dry:
A creature might forget to weep, who bore
Thy comfort long, and lose thy love thereby!
But love me for love's sake, that evermore
Thou mayst love on, through love's eternity.

Elizabeth Barrett Browning (1806–61), *Sonnets from the
Portuguese*

Love will never come to an end

If I speak in the tongues of mortals and of angels, but do not have love, I am a noisy gong or a clanging cymbal. And if I have prophetic powers, and understand all mysteries and all knowledge, and if I have all faith, so as to remove mountains, but do not have love, I am nothing. If I give away all my possessions, and if I hand over my body so that I may boast, but do not have love, I gain nothing.

Love is patient; love is kind; love is not envious or boastful or arrogant or rude. It does not insist on its own way; it is not irritable or resentful; it does not rejoice in wrongdoing, but rejoices in the truth. It bears all things, believes all things, hopes all things, endures all things.

Love never ends. But as for prophecies, they will come to an end; as for tongues, they will cease; as for knowledge, it will come to an end. For we know only in part, and we prophesy only in part; but when the complete comes, the partial will come to an end. When I was a child, I spoke like a child, I thought like a child, I reasoned like a child; when I became an adult, I put an end to childish ways. For now we see in a mirror, dimly, but then we will see face to face. Now I know only in part; then I will know fully, even as I have been fully known. And now faith, hope and love abide, these three; and the greatest of these is love.

First Letter of St Paul to the Corinthians 13, the Bible

Love bade me welcome

Love bade me welcome: yet my soul drew back,
      Guilty of dust and sin.
But quick-ey'd Love, observing me grow slack
      From my first entrance in,
Drew nearer to me, sweetly questioning,
      If I lack'd any thing.

A guest, I answer'd, worthy to be here:
      Love said, You shall be he.
I the unkind, ungrateful? Ah my dear,
      I cannot look on thee.
Love took my hand, and smiling did reply,
      Who made the eyes but I?

Truth Lord, but I have marr'd them: let my shame
      Go where it doth deserve.
And know you not, says Love, who bore the blame?
      My dear, then I will serve.
You must sit down, says Love, and taste my meat:
      So I did sit and eat.

George Herbert (1593–1633)

Love

When you love, you should not say, 'God is in my heart,' but rather, 'I am in the heart of God.'
And think not you can direct the course of love, for love, if it finds you worthy, directs your course.

Love has no other desire but to fulfill itself.
But if you love and must needs have desires, let these be your desires:
To melt and be like a running brook that sings its melody to the night.
To know the pain of too much tenderness.
To be wounded by your own understanding of love;
And to bleed willingly and joyfully.
To wake at dawn with a winged heart and give thanks for another day of loving;
To rest at the noon hour and meditate love's ecstasy;
To return home at eventide with gratitude;
And then to sleep with a prayer for the beloved in your heart and a song of praise upon your lips.

Khalil Gibran (1883–1931), *The Prophet*

The bargain

My true-love hath my heart, and I have his,
     By just exchange one to the other given:
I hold his dear, and mine he cannot miss,
     There never was a better bargain driven:
His heart in me keeps him and me in one,
     My heart in him his thoughts and senses guides:
He loves my heart, for once it was his own,
     I cherish his because in me it bides.
His heart his wound received from my sight,
     My heart was wounded with his wounded heart;
For as from me on him his hurt did light,
     So still methought in me his hurt did smart.
          Both equal hurt, in this change sought our bliss:
          My true love hath my heart and I have his.

Sir Philip Sidney (1554–86)

True friendship

You should pay attention to the various steps which
lead to the summit of perfect friendship. A person
ought first to be chosen, next tested, and only then finally
admitted into friendship, and from then on treated as a
true friend deserves. Now when I speak about choosing
our friends, I advise that you exclude from consideration
those who are quarrelsome, irascible, fickle, suspicious,
or who can't stop talking. Yet not all these, but only

those who are unable or unwilling to regulate or change their behaviour in the service of true friendship.

There are four qualities which must be tested in a friend: loyalty, good intentions, discretion and patience. Only then can you entrust yourself to a friend securely. You must look for the right intention, so that he expects nothing from your friendship except God and its natural good. A friend should be discreet, so that he may understand what is to be done on behalf of your friendship and what is not; what are appropriate expectations of your friendship; and what sufferings are to be endured in the course of it. For your part, you should be ready to congratulate him on his successes, but not draw back from pointing out any short-comings. Finally, a friend should be patient, not sulking if you challenge him, or worse, despising or hating you for daring to criticize him. True friends are always willing to bear difficulties for the sake of the other.

Above all, there is nothing more praiseworthy in friendship than loyalty, which seems to be its nurse and guardian. It proves itself a true companion in all situations: adversity and prosperity, joy and sadness, fun and stress. Loyalty views other people equally. The humble and the lofty, the poor and the rich, the strong and the weak, the healthy and the infirm, are all seen with the same eye.

A truly loyal friend sees nothing in his friend but his heart.

Aelred of Rievaulx (1109–67), *On Spiritual Friendship*

A word to husbands

To keep your marriage brimming,
    With love in the loving cup,
Whenever you're wrong, admit it;
Whenever you're right, shut up.

Ogden Nash (1902–71)

A red, red rose

My love is like a red, red rose
    That's newly sprung in June:
My love is like the melody
    That's sweetly played in tune.

As fair art thou, my bonnie lass,
    So deep in love am I:
And I will love thee still, my dear,
    Till a' the seas gang dry.

Till a' the seas gang dry, my dear,
    And the rocks melt wi' the sun:
And I will love thee still, my dear,
    While the sands o' life shall run.

And fare thee weel, my only love,
    And fare thee weel a while!
And I will come again, my love,
    Thou' it were ten thousand mile.

Robert Burns (1759–96)

The Owl and the Pussy-Cat

The Owl and the Pussy-Cat went to sea
   In a beautiful pea-green boat,
They took some honey, and plenty of money,
   Wrapped up in a five-pound note.
The Owl looked up to the stars above,
   And sang to a small guitar,
'O lovely Pussy! O Pussy, my love,
   What a beautiful Pussy you are,
       You are,
       You are!
   What a beautiful Pussy you are!'

Pussy said to the Owl, 'You elegant fowl!
   How charmingly sweet you sing!
O let us be married! Too long we have tarried:
   But what shall we do for a ring?'
They sailed away for a year and a day,
   To the land where the Bong-tree grows,
And there in a wood a Piggy-wig stood,
   With a ring at the end of his nose,
       His nose,
       His nose,
   With a ring at the end of his nose.

'Dear Pig, are you willing to sell for one shilling
   Your ring?' Said the Piggy, 'I will.'
So they took it away, and were married next day
   By the Turkey who lives on the hill.
They dined on mince, and slices of quince,
   Which they ate with a runcible spoon;

And hand in hand, on the edge of the sand,
   They danced by the light of the moon,
      The moon,
      The moon,
   They danced by the light of the moon.

Edward Lear (1812–88)

The good-morrow

I wonder by my troth, what thou, and I
  Did, till we lov'd? Were we not wean'd till then?
But suck'd on country pleasures, childishly?
Or snorted we i'the seven sleepers den?
'Twas so; But this, all pleasures fancies be.
If ever any beauty I did see,
Which I desir'd, and got, 'twas but a dream of thee.

And now good-morrow to our waking souls,
Which watch not one another out of fear;
For love, all love of other sights controls,
And makes one little room, an everywhere.
Let sea-discoverers to new worlds have gone,
Let maps to others, worlds on worlds have shown,
Let us possess our world, each hath one, and is one.

My face is thine eye, thine in mine appears,
And true plain hearts do in the faces rest,
Where can we find two better hemispheres
Without sharp North, without declining West?

Whatever dies, was not mixed equally;
If our two loves be one, or thou and I
Love so alike, that none do slacken, none can die.

John Donne (1572–1631)

Let love be genuine

L et love be genuine; hate what is evil, hold fast to what is good; love one another with mutual affection; outdo one another in showing honour. Do not lag in zeal, be ardent in spirit, serve the Lord. Rejoice in hope, be patient in suffering, persevere in prayer. Contribute to the needs of the saints; extend hospitality to strangers.

Bless those who persecute you; bless and do not curse them. Rejoice with those who rejoice, weep with those who weep. Live in harmony with one another; do not be haughty, but associate with the lowly; do not claim to be wiser than you are. Do not repay anyone evil for evil, but take thought for what is noble in the sight of all. If it is possible, so far as it depends on you, live peaceably with all.

St Paul's Letter to the Romans 12, the Bible

Love as the giving of self

A person who loves holds nothing for himself: he reserves nothing as of right. That which he holds, he holds either on trust or as gift.

The enrichment which many discover in the experience of loving is not an enlargement of rights or an increase in possession: it is the discovery as trust or gift of that which had previously been known only as possession. When a person loves, all that is in their power is invested with a sense of purpose, as available for the other, or becomes a cause or occasion of gratitude, as received by gift from the other.

The falsity of love is exposed wherever any limit is set by the will of those who profess to love: wherever, by their will something is withheld. Therefore the authenticity of love must imply a totality of giving – that which we call the giving of self or self-giving. The self is the totality of what a person has and is: and it is no less than this that is offered or made available in love. When we become aware that something less than the self is offered, we become aware of the falsity of love.

W. H. Vanstone, *Love's Endeavour, Love's Expense*

I love you

I love you,
   Not only for what you are,
But for what I am
When I am with you.

I love you,
Not only for what
You have made of yourself.
But for what
You are making of me.

I love you
For the part of me
That you bring out;
I love you
For putting your hand
Into my heaped-up heart
And passing over
All the foolish, weak things
That you can't help
Dimly seeing there,
And for drawing out
Into the light
All the beautiful belongings
That no one else had looked
Quite far enough to find.

I love you because you
Are helping me to make
Of the lumber of my life
Not a tavern
But a temple;
Out of the works
Of my every day
Not a reproach
But a song.

I love you
Because you have done
More than any creed
Could have done
To make me good,
And more than any fate
Could have done
To make me happy.

You have done it
Without a touch
Without a word
Without a sign.
You have done it
By being yourself.
Perhaps that is what
Being a friend means,
After all.

Roy Croft (1907–73)

Love, sex and intimacy

'God is friendship. What is true of charity, I surely do not hesitate to grant to friendship, since "he that abides in friendship, abides in God, and God in him."' These words of Aelred, the twelfth-century Yorkshire Cistercian, in his wonderful book on friendship, remind us that it is important not to reduce our understanding of sexuality to genital activity, as if this one area provides the total meaning of love and intimacy. Sexuality, in its broadest sense, covers our whole experience of embodiment. Affective sexuality involves a huge area of feelings and emotions that move us towards other people. And this is true of all kinds of relationships, including those of single people. It is, if you like, what enables all of us to express tenderness, closeness, compassion and openness to touch. It follows that intimacy is not something reserved to certain categories of people (that is, the married) and not to others. Single people, including those committed for various reasons to celibacy, are equally called to intimacy with other human beings.

Philip Sheldrake, *Befriending our Desires*

The undertaking

I have done one braver thing
 Than all the *Worthies* did,
Yet a braver thence doth spring,
 Which is, to keep that hid.

It were but madness now to impart
 The skill of specular stone.
When he which can have learned the art
 To cut it, can find none.

So, if I now should utter this,
 Others (because no more
Such stuff to work upon, there is,)
 Would love but as before.

But he who loveliness within
 Hath found, all outward loathes;
For he who colour loves, and skin,
 Loves but their oldest clothes.

If, as I have, you also do
 Virtue attired in woman see,
And dare love that, and say so too,
 And forget the He and She;

And if this love, though placed so,
 From profane men you hide,
Which will no faith on this bestow,
 Or, if they do, deride:

Then you've done a braver thing
Than all the *Worthies* did;
And a braver thence will spring,
Which is, to keep that hid.

John Donne (1572–1631)

Let me not to the marriage of true minds

Let me not to the marriage of true minds
  Admit impediments. Love is not love
Which alters when it alteration finds,
  Or bends with the remover to remove.
O, no! it is an ever-fixèd mark,
  That looks on tempests and is never shaken;
It is the star to every wandering bark,
  Whose worth's unknown, although his height be
    taken.
Love's not Time's fool, though rosy lips and cheeks
  Within his bending sickle's compass come;
Love alters not with his brief hours and weeks,
  But bears it out even to the edge of doom.
    If this be error, and upon me proved,
    I never writ, nor no man ever loved.

William Shakespeare (1564–1616), Sonnet CXVI

Marriage

Then Almitra spoke again and said, And what of
  Marriage, master?
And he answered saying:
You were born together, and together you shall be
  for evermore.
You shall be together when the white wings of death
  scatter your days.
Aye, you shall be together even in the silent memory
  of God.
But let there be spaces in your togetherness.
And let the winds of the heavens dance between you.

Love one another, but make not a bond of love:
Let it rather be a moving sea between the shores of
  your souls.
Fill each other's cup but drink not from one cup.
Give one another of your bread but eat not from the
  same loaf.
Sing and dance together and be joyous, but let each
  one of you be alone,
Even as the strings of a lute are alone though they
  quiver with the same music.

Give your hearts, but not into each other's keeping.
For only the hand of Life can contain your hearts.
And stand together yet not too near together:
For the pillars of the temple stand apart,
And the oak tree and the cypress grow not in each
  other's shadow.

Khalil Gibran (1883–1931), *The Prophet*

Fear has no place in marriage

Nothing is stronger than bonds of love, particularly between husband and wife. If you resort to intimidation you might succeed in keeping a servant attached to you for a while, but in all probability the servant will leave you and run away at the first opportunity. But the companion of your life, the mother of your children, the ground of your joy, ought she be tied to you by threats and fear? Surely, only by love and cherishing? What sort of union is it where a wife is petrified of her husband? And what pleasure is there for her husband in tyrannising his wife as if she were a slave instead of respecting her dignity as a free woman?

Two souls united in love should have nothing to fear either in the present or the future. For where there is harmony, peace and mutuality of love, then husband and wife already possess everything that is good.

St John Chrysostom (347–407)

Perfect love casts out fear

Beloved, let us love one another, because love is from God; everyone who loves is born of God and knows God. Whoever does not love does not know God, for God is love. God's love was revealed among us in this way: God sent his only Son into the world so that we might live through him. In this is love, not that we loved

God but that he loved us and sent his Son to be the aton-
ing sacrifice for our sins. Beloved, since God loved us so
much, we also ought to love one another. No one has
ever seen God: if we love one another, God lives in us,
and his love is perfected in us.

God is love, and those who abide in love abide in God,
and God abides in them. There is no fear in love, but perfect love casts out fear.

The First Letter of St John 4, the Bible

A prayer for success

Lord, behold our family here assembled.
　　We thank thee for this place in which we dwell;
　for the love that unites us;
For the peace accorded us this day; for the hope with
　　which we expect the morrow;
For the health, the work, the food, and the bright skies,
　　that make our lives delightful;
For our friends in all parts of the earth;
Purge out of every heart the lurking grudge.
Give us grace and strength to forbear and to persevere.
Forgetful ourselves, help us to bear cheerfully the
　　forgetfulness of others.
Give us courage and gaiety and a quiet mind.
Spare to us our friends, soften to us our enemies.
Bless us, if it may be, in all our innocent endeavours.
If it may not, give us the strength to encounter that
　　which is to come,

That we may be brave in peril, constant in tribulation,
    temperate in wrath,
And in all changes of fortune, and down to the gates
    of death,
Loyal and loving one to another.
As the clay to the potter, as the windmill to the wind,
We beseech of thee this help and mercy,
    for Christ's sake.

Robert Louis Stevenson (1850–94), from his memorial by
Augustus Saint-Gaudens, in St Giles' Cathedral, Edinburgh

A blessing of a marriage

God of tenderness and strength,
    in your loving wisdom
you have brought together N and N
and led them to this day:
pour upon them the abundance of your blessing
as they begin married life together.
Let their love for each other be a seal upon their hearts
and a crown upon their heads.
Travel with them in the years ahead;
uphold them in good times and in bad;
sustain them in times of sadness and disappointment;
and by your grace,
may they always be tender with each other's dreams.

Anonymous

With this ring I thee wed

The wedding ring

The ring so worn, as you behold,
  So thin, so pale, is yet of gold:
The passion such it was to prove;
Worn with life's cares, love yet was love.

George Crabbe (1754–1832)

To my dear and loving husband

If ever two were one, then surely we.
  If ever man were lov'd by wife, then thee;
If ever wife was happy in a man,
Compare with me ye women if you can.
I prize thy love more than whole mines of gold,
Or all the riches that the East doth hold.
My love is such that rivers cannot quench,
Nor aught but love from thee, give recompense.
Thy love is such I can no way repay,
The heavens reward thee manifold, I pray.
Then while we live, in love lets so persever
That, when we live no more, we may live ever.

Anne Bradstreet (1612–72)

Clothe yourselves with compassion and love

As God's chosen ones, holy and beloved, clothe yourselves with compassion, kindness, humility, meekness and patience. Bear with one another and, if anyone has a complaint against another, forgive each other; just as the Lord has forgiven you, so you also must forgive. Above all, clothe yourselves with love, which binds everything together in perfect harmony. And let the peace of Christ rule in your hearts, to which indeed you were called in the one body. And be thankful. Let the word of Christ dwell in you richly; teach and admonish one another in all wisdom; and with gratitude in your hearts sing psalms, hymns, and spiritual songs to God. And whatever you do, in word or deed, do everything in the name of the Lord Jesus, giving thanks to God the Father through him.

St Paul's Letter to the Colossians 3, the Bible

O perfect love

O perfect Love, all human thought transcending,
　　Lowly we kneel in prayer before thy throne,
That theirs may be the love that knows no ending
　　Whom thou for evermore dost join in one.

O perfect Life, be thou their full assurance
　　Of tender charity and steadfast faith,
Of patient hope, and quiet brave endurance,
　　With childlike trust that fears nor pain nor death.

Grant them the joy that brightens earthly sorrow,
   Grant them the peace which calms all earthly strife;
And to life's day the glorious unknown morrow
   That dawns upon eternal love and life.

Dorothy F. Gurney (1858–1932)

Love song

How can I keep my soul in me, so that
it doesn't touch your soul? How can I raise
it high enough, past you, to other things?
I would like to shelter it, among remote
lost objects, in some dark and silent place
that doesn't resonate when your depths resound.
Yet everything that touches us, me and you,
takes us together like a violin's bow,
which draws one voice out of two separate strings.
Upon what instrument are we two spanned?
And what musician holds us in his hand?
Oh! sweetest song.

Rainer Maria Rilke (1875–1926), translated by Stephen
Mitchell

A Celtic blessing

Deep peace of the running wave to you,

Deep peace of the flowing air to you,

Deep peace of the quiet earth to you,

Deep peace of the shining stars to you,

Deep peace of the Son of Peace to you.

Anonymous

An Apache blessing

Now you will feel no rain,
for each of you will be a shelter to the other.

Now you will feel no cold,
for each of you will be warmth to the other.

Now there will be no loneliness,
for each of you will be a comfort to the other.

Now you are two persons,
but there is only one life before you.

Go now to your dwelling place,
to enter into the days of your togetherness.

And may your days be good
and long upon the earth.

Anonymous

Love divine

Love divine, all loves excelling,
    Joy of heaven, to earth come down,
Fix in us thy humble dwelling,
    All thy faithful mercies crown.
Jesu, thou art all compassion,
    Pure unbounded love thou art;
Visit us with thy salvation,
    Enter every trembling heart.

Come, almighty to deliver,
    Let us all thy life receive;
Suddenly return, and never,
    Never more thy temples leave.
Thee we would be always blessing,
    Serve thee as thy hosts above,
Pray, and praise thee, without ceasing,
    Glory in thy perfect love.

Finish then thy new creation,
    Pure and spotless let us be;
Let us see thy great salvation,
    Perfectly restored in thee,
Changed from glory into glory,
    Till in heaven we take our place,
Till we cast our crowns before thee,
    Lost in wonder, love, and praise.

Charles Wesley (1703–91)

Wild nights

Wild Nights – Wild Nights!
　　Were I with thee,
Wild Nights should be
Our luxury!

Futile – the Winds –
To a Heart in port –
Done with the Compass –
Done with the Chart!

Rowing in Eden –
Ah, the Sea!
Might I but moor – Tonight –
In thee!

Emily Dickinson (1830–86)

My wife

Trusty, dusky, vivid, true,
　　With eyes of gold and bramble-dew,
Steel true and blade-straight,
The great artificer
Made my mate.

Honour, anger, valour, fire,
A love that life could never tire,
Death quench or evil stir;
The mighty master
Gave to her.

Teacher, tender, comrade, wife,
A fellow-farer true through life,
Heart-whole and soul-free,
The august father
Gave to me.

Robert Louis Stevenson (1850–94)

I do, I will, I have

How wise I am to have instructed the butler to
instruct the first footman to instruct the second
footman to instruct the doorman to order my
carriage;
I am about to volunteer a definition of marriage.
Just as I know that there are two Hagens, Walter and
Copen,
I know that marriage is a legal and religious alliance
entered into by a man who can't sleep with the
window shut and a woman who can't sleep with
the window open.
Moreover, just as I am unsure of the difference between
flora and fauna and flotsam and jetsam,
I am quite sure that marriage is the alliance of two
people one of whom never remembers birthdays
and the other never forgetsam,
And he refuses to believe there is a leak in the water
pipe or the gas pipe and she is convinced she is
about to asphyxiate or drown,

And she says Quick get up and get my hairbrushes off
       the windowsill, it's raining in, and he replies Oh
       they're all right, it's only raining straight down.
That is why marriage is so much more interesting than
       divorce,
Because it's the only known example of the happy
       meeting of the immovable object and the
       irresistible force.
So I hope husbands and wives will continue to debate
       and combat over everything debatable and
       combatable,
Because I believe a little incompatibility is the spice of
life, particularly if he has income and she is pattable.

Ogden Nash (1902–71)

For each ecstatic instant

For each ecstatic instant
    We must an anguish pay.
In keen and quivering ratio
To the ecstasy.

For each beloved hour
Sharp pittances of years,
Bitter contested farthings
And coffers heaped with tears.

Emily Dickinson (1830–86)

In search of intimacy

The call to intimacy that we all experience at different points in our lives is an invitation to take risks. For all human love can come to an end, may deceive, is partial, is not totally and finally reliable. Yet our capacity and need for intimacy is a call to find within this risk of human loving the love of God that is total, constant and faithful. Deep human friendship is a powerful contribution, arguably the most powerful, to a loving union with God. The call to intimacy also involves a realisation that however much two people love each other they will never possess or own each other nor will they ever fully know each other. There is always an area of inalienable strangeness in the other person. There is, therefore, for ever the possibility of greater depth, of 'more', in all relationships.

Whether we are single or in a committed, exclusive relationship, to become complete we are all called to seek the eventual integration of particular love (*eros*) and universal love (*agape*). Only within our experiences of intimacy with other people, whether genital or not, may we learn a way of being fully present both to ourselves and to others rather than being superficial and remote in our emotional lives. The risk of intimacy, rather than the apparent security of emotional detachment, reveals the truth of ourselves, teaches us about availability, educates us in truthful self-disclosure and of all human experiences is the one most likely to provoke real change in us.

Philip Sheldrake, *Befriending Our Desires*

Forsaking all others

So, we'll go no more a-roving

So, we'll go no more a-roving
   So late into the night,
Though the heart be still as loving,
   And the moon be still as bright.

For the sword outwears its sheath,
   And the soul wears out the breast,
And the heart must pause to breathe,
   And love itself have rest.

Though the night was made for loving,
   And the day returns too soon,
Yet we'll go no more a-roving
   By the light of the moon.

Lord Byron (1788–1824)

O never say that I was false of heart

O never say that I was false of heart,
   Though absence seemed my flame to qualify.
As easy might I from myself depart
   As from my soul, which in thy breast doth lie:
That is my home of love; if I have ranged,
   Like him that travels, I return again,
Just to the time, not with the time exchanged,
   So that myself bring water for my stain.
Never believe, though in my nature reigned
   All frailties that besiege all kinds of blood,
That it could so preposterously be stained,
   To leave for nothing all thy sum of good;
     For nothing this wide universe I call,
     Save thou, my rose; in it thou art my all.

William Shakespeare (1564–1616), Sonnet CIX

Deceit is the enemy of good relationships

Every lie constitutes a sin. It is a sin, not only when we know the truth and blatantly lie, but also when we are mistaken and deceived in what we say. It remains our duty to speak what we think in our heart, whether it be true, or we just think that it's true. A liar says the opposite of what he thinks in his heart, because his purpose is to deceive others.

We have been given the gift of speech not to deceive one another, but to communicate truthfully with each other. To use speech for the purpose of deception is to pervert its purpose and is wrong. Nor should we kid ourselves that there are some lies that are not sinful, because (we suppose) in telling a lie we are doing someone a service. For example, you could make an argument for committing adultery. If I don't sleep with this woman, you say to yourself, she will die of love for me. Your action is no less wrong. If we value marital fidelity, refusing to countenance anything that will undermine a marriage, how is it that we are quite happy to undermine a relationship by lying?

Let us be true heirs of the new covenant, to whom our Lord Jesus said: 'Let your Yes be Yes, and your No, No; for whatever else comes from the evil One.' It is on account of our many failures in this regard, failures which never cease to creep into our living, that we cry out to God: 'Lord, forgive us our sins.'

St Augustine (354–430), *The Enchiridion*

Freedom and Love

How delicious is the winning
   Of a kiss at love's beginning,
When two mutual hearts are sighing
For the knot there's no untying!

Yet remember, 'midst our wooing,
Love has bliss, but Love has ruing;
Other smiles may make you fickle,
Tears for other charms may trickle.

Love he comes, and Love he tarries,
Just as fate or fancy carries;
Longest stays, when sorest chidden;
Laughs and flies, when press'd and bidden.

Bind the sea to slumber stilly,
Bind its odour to the lily,
Bind the aspen ne'er to quiver,
Then bind Love to last for ever.

Love's a fire that needs renewal
Of fresh beauty for its fuel:
Love's wing moults when caged and captured,
Only free, he soars enraptured.

Can you keep the bee from ranging
Or the ringdove's neck from changing?
No! nor fetter'd Love from dying
In the knot there's no untying.

Thomas Campbell (1777–1844)

Love and the acceptance of restraint

Among the circumstances which restrict the expression of love is the capacity of the other to receive. A parent knows the danger of overwhelming or imprisoning a child by expressions of love which are untimely or excessive. A friend knows that expressions of friendship too sudden or demonstrative may simply embarrass. A wife knows that, out of love for her husband, she must sometimes 'think about herself'.

The external restraint which love practises is often a mark of its freedom from internal limit. Love does not lay down the condition that it must be allowed freedom to express itself, nor limit its activity to those circumstances in which it may freely act. Love accepts without limit the discipline of circumstances. Although it always aspires to enlarge its own activity, it sometimes finds its most generous enlargement in the acceptance of restraint. Love must sometimes express itself in the renunciation of not disclosing itself. That which love withholds is withheld for the sake of the other who is loved – so that it may not harm them, so that it may be used for a more timely service or so that it may mature into a richer gift.

W. H. Vanstone, *Love's Endeavour, Love's Expense*

I love thee

I love thee – I love thee!
　'Tis all that I can say;
It is my vision in the night,
　My dreaming in the day;
The very echo of my heart,
　The blessing when I pray:
I love thee – I love thee,
　Is all that I can say.

I love thee – I love thee!
　Is ever on my tongue;
In all my proudest poesy
　That chorus still is sung;
It is the verdict of my eyes,
　Amidst the gay and young:
I love thee – I love thee!
　A thousand maids among.

I love thee – I love thee!
　Thy bright and hazel glance,
The mellow lute upon those lips,
　Whose tender tones entrance;
But most, dear heart of hearts, thy proofs
　That still these words enhance,
I love thee – I love thee!
　Whatever be thy chance.

Thomas Hood (1799–1845)

Double standards

Some people think that while it is wrong for women to have sexual relations before marriage, it is perfectly acceptable for men to do so. This licentiousness is wrong, made worse by the fact that some men's behaviour has become so habitual that in the eyes of many people their actions are viewed as inconsequential and trivial, nothing serious. Now in Christian teaching there can be no double-standards. Whatever is unlawful for a woman is equally unlawful for a man.

Let me point out another wrong. How is it that many men are quite happy to live with various women before they marry, but suddenly, when it suits them, they get rid of these poor women in order to contract a more advantageous marriage? Before God and his angels I attest and declare that God condemns such behaviour and in no way approves of such actions. It never has been and never shall be lawful to behave in this way. Men who do this may claim the authority of the market place for their behaviour, but they do not enjoy the authority of heaven. They are controlled by lust, whereas they should be ordering their lives according to justice.

St Caesarius of Arles (c.470–543)

In sickness and in health

Love, marriage and perseverance

People get from books the idea that if you have married the right person you may expect to go on 'being in love' for ever. As a result, when they find they are not, they think this proves they have made a mistake and are entitled to a change – not realising that, when they have changed, the glamour will presently go out of the new love just as it went out of the old one. In this department of life, as in every other, thrills come at the beginning and do not last.

Let the thrill go – let it die away – go on through that period of death into the quieter interest and happiness that follow – and you will find you are living in a world of new thrills all the time. But if you decide to make thrills your regular diet and try to prolong them artificially, they will all get weaker and weaker, and fewer and fewer, and you will be a bored, disillusioned old man for the rest of your life. It is because so few people understand this that you find many middle-aged men and women maundering about their lost youth, at the very age when new horizons ought to be appearing and new doors opening all round them. It is much better fun to learn to swim than to go on endlessly (and hope-lessly) trying to get back the feeling you had when you first went paddling as a small boy.

C. S. Lewis (1898–1963), *Mere Christianity*

What makes a good marriage?

A good marriage is one in which each appoints the other guardian of his or her solitude, and shows him this confidence, the greatest in his power to bestow.

Once the realisation is accepted that even between the *closest* human beings infinite distances continue to exist, a wonderful living side by side can grow up, if they succeed in loving the distance between them which makes it possible for each to see the other whole and against a wide sky.

Rainer Maria Rilke (1875–1926), *Letters to a Young Poet*

The perfect husband

He tells you when you've got on
        too much lipstick
And helps you with your girdle
        when your hips stick.

Ogden Nash (1902–71)

Do not worry about tomorrow

Jesus said to his disciples, 'Do not worry about your life, what you will eat or what you will drink, or about your body, what you will wear. Is not life more than food, and the body more than clothing? Look at the birds of the air; they neither sow nor reap nor gather into barns, and yet your heavenly Father feeds them. Are you not of more value than they?

And can any of you by worrying add a single hour to the span of your life? And why do you worry about clothing? Consider the lilies of the field, how they grow; they neither toil nor spin, yet I tell you, even Solomon in all his glory was not clothed like one of these. But if God so clothes the grass of the field, which is alive today and tomorrow is thrown into the oven, will he not much more clothe you – you of little faith?

Therefore do not worry, saying, 'What will we eat?' or 'What will we drink?' or 'What will we wear?' For it is the Gentiles who strive for all these things; and indeed your heavenly Father knows that you need all these things. But strive first for the kingdom of God and his righteousness, and all these things will be given to you as well. So do not worry about tomorrow, for tomorrow will bring worries of its own. Today's trouble is enough for today.

St Matthew's Gospel 6, the Bible

The loom of time

Man's life is laid in the loom of time
 To a pattern he does not see,
While the weavers work and the shuttles fly
 Till the dawn of eternity.

Some shuttles are filled with silver threads
 And some with threads of gold,
While often but the darker hues
 Are all that they may hold.

But the weaver watches with skilful eye
 Each shuttle fly to and fro,
And sees the pattern so deftly wrought
 As the loom moves sure and slow.

God surely planned the pattern:
 Each thread, the dark and fair,
Is chosen by his master skill
 And placed in the web with care.

He only knows its beauty,
 And guides the shuttles which hold
The threads so unattractive,
 As well as the threads of gold.

Not till the loom is silent,
 And the shuttles cease to fly,
Shall God reveal the pattern
 And explain the reason why

The dark threads were as needful
 In the weaver's skilful hand
As the threads of gold and silver
 For the pattern which he planned.

Anonymous

Love is a sickness

Love is a sickness full of woes,
 All remedies refusing;
A plant that with most cutting grows,
 Most barren with best using.
  Why so?
More we enjoy it, more it dies;
If not enjoyed, its sighing cries
  Heigh ho!
Love is a torment of the mind,
 A tempest everlasting;
And Jove hath made it of a kind
 Not well, nor full, nor fasting.
  Why so?
More we enjoy it, more it dies;
If not enjoyed, its sighing cries
  Heigh ho!

Samuel Daniel (1562–1619)

The joyous malingerer

Who is the happy husband? Why, indeed,
    'Tis he who's useless in the time of need;
Who, asked to unclasp a bracelet or a neckless,
Contrives to be utterly futile, fumbling, feckless,
Or when a zipper nips his loved one's back
Cannot restore the zipper to its track.
Another time, not wishing to be flayed,
She will not use him as a lady's maid.

Stove-wise he's the perpetual backward learner
Who can't turn on or off the proper burner.
If faced with washing up he never gripes,
But simply drops more dishes than he wipes.
She finds his absence preferable to his aid,
And thus all mealtime chores doth he evade.

He can, attempting to replace a fuse,
Black out the coast from Boston to Newport News,
Or, hanging pictures, be the rookie wizard
Who fills the parlor with a plaster blizzard.
He'll not again be called to competition
With decorator or with electrician.

At last it dawns upon his patient spouse
He's better at his desk than round the house.

Ogden Nash (1902–71)

When my love swears that she is made of truth

When my love swears that she is made of truth
 I do believe her, though I know she lies,
That she might think me some untutor'd youth
 Unlearned in the world's false subtleties.
Thus vainly thinking that she thinks me young,
 Although she knows my days are past my best,
Simply I credit her false-speaking tongue;
 On both sides thus is simple truth suppressed.
But wherefore says she not she is unjust?
 And wherefore say not I that I am old?
O that love's best habit is in seeming trust,
 And age in love loves not to have years told.
Therefore I lie with her, and she with me,
 And in our faults by lies we flattered be.

William Shakespeare (1564–1616), Sonnet CXXXVIII

The bungler

You glow in my heart
 Like the flames of uncounted candles.
 But when I go to warm my hands,
 My clumsiness overturns the light
  And then I stumble
 Against the tables and chairs.

Amy Lowell (1874–1925)

Prayer for a new beginning

God of new beginnings,
   you look on us with pity, not with blame.
Forgive our failures and renew our hope.
Help us not to harbour resentment
or to nurse a grudge,
but to let go of past hurts,
that memories can begin to heal
and trust be renewed.
Give us grace
to be tender with each other's dreams,
and once again to walk hand in hand.

Anonymous

Till death us do part

The bride

My love looks like a girl tonight,
    But she is old.
The plaits that lie along her pillow
Are not gold,
But threaded with filigree silver,
And uncanny gold.

She looks like a young maiden, since her brow
Is smooth and fair,
Her cheeks are very smooth, her eyes are closed,
She sleeps a rare
Still winsome sleep, so still, and so composed.

Nay, but she sleeps like a bride, and dreams her dreams
Of perfect things.
She lies at last, the darling, in the shape of her dream,
And her dead mouth sings
By its shape, like the thrushes in clear evenings.

D. H. Lawrence (1885–1930)

How do I love thee? Let me count the ways

How do I love thee? Let me count the ways.
   I love thee to the depth and breadth and height
My soul can reach, when feeling out of sight
For the ends of being and ideal grace.
I love thee to the level of every day's
Most quiet need, by sun and candlelight.
I love thee freely, as men strive for right;
I love thee purely, as they turn from praise.
I love thee with the passion put to use
In my old griefs, and with my childhood's faith.
I love thee with a love I seemed to lose
With my lost saints – I love thee with the breath,
Smiles, tears, of all my life! – and, if God choose,
I shall but love thee better after death.

Elizabeth Barrett Browning (1806–61),
Sonnets from the Portuguese

The hill

Breathless, we flung us on the windy hill,
   Laughed in the sun, and kissed the lovely grass.
   You said, 'Through glory and ecstasy we pass;
Wind, sun, and earth remain, the birds sing still,
When we are old, are old . . .' 'And when we die
All's over that is ours; and life burns on
Through other lovers, other lips,' said I,
'Heart of my heart, our heaven is now, is won!'

'We are Earth's best, that learnt her lesson here.
   Life is our cry. We have kept the faith!' we said;
   'We shall go down with unreluctant tread
Rose-crowned into the darkness!' . . . Proud we were,
And laughed, that had such brave true things to say.
– And then you suddenly cried, and turned away.

Rupert Brooke (1887–1915)

While over there

Seventeen years ago you said
    Something that sounded like Goodbye;
    And everybody thinks that you are dead,
        But I.

So I, as I grow stiff and cold
    To this and that say Goodbye too;
    And everybody sees that I am old
        But you.

    And one fine morning in a sunny lane
Some boy and girl will meet and kiss and swear
    That nobody can love their way again,
        While over there
You will have smiled, I shall have tossed your hair.

Charlotte Mew (1869–1928)

They that love beyond the world

They that love beyond the world, cannot be sepa-
rated. Death cannot kill what never dies. Nor can
spirits ever be divided that love and live in the same
Divine Principle; the root and record of their friendship.
Death is but crossing the world, as friends do the seas;
they live in one another still.

William Penn (1644–1718), *Fruits of Solitude*

These I can promise

I cannot promise you a life of sunshine;
I cannot promise riches, wealth or gold;
I cannot promise you an easy pathway
That leads away from change or growing old.

But I can promise all my heart's devotion
A smile to chase away your tears of sorrow;
A love that's ever true and ever growing;
A hand to hold in yours through each tomorrow.

Mark Twain (1835–1910)

Till death breaks the record

The particular charm of marriage is the duologue, the permanent conversation between two people who talk over everything and everyone, till death breaks the record. It is this back-chat which, in the long run, makes a reciprocal equality more intoxicating than any form of servitude or domination.

Cyril Connolly (1903–74), *The Unquiet Grave*

The anniversary

All Kings, and all their favourites,
  All glory of honours, beauties, wits,
The sun itself, which makes times, as they pass,
Is elder by a year now than it was
When thou and I first one another saw:
All other things to their destruction draw,
  Only our love hath no decay;
This no tomorrow hath, nor yesterday,
Running it never runs from us away,
But truly keeps his first, last, everlasting day.

Two graves must hide thine and my course;
  If one might, death were no divorce.
Alas, as well as other Princes, we
(Who Prince enough in one another be)
Must leave at last in death these eyes and ears,
Oft fed with true oaths, and with sweet salt tears;
  But souls where nothing dwells but love
(All other thoughts being inmates) then shall prove
This, or a love increased there above,
When bodies to their graves, souls from their
      graves remove.

And then we shall be thoroughly blest;
  But we no more than all the rest.
Here upon earth we're Kings, and none but we
Can be such Kings, nor of such subjects be;
Who is so safe as we? Where none can do
Treason to us, except one of us two.

True and false fears let us refrain,
Let us love nobly, and live, and add again
Years and years unto years, till we attain
To write threescore: this is the second of our reign.

John Donne (1572–1631)

Enjoying the world

Your enjoyment of the world is never right till every morning you awake in heaven; see yourself in your Father's palace; and look upon the skies, the earth, and the air as celestial joys having such a reverend esteem of all as if you were among the angels. The bride of a monarch in her husband's chamber hath no such causes of delight as you.

You never enjoy the world aright till the sea itself floweth in your veins, till you are clothed with the heavens, and crowned with the stars, and perceive yourself to be the sole heir of the whole world, and more than so, because men are in it who are every one sole heirs as well as you. Till you can sing and rejoice and delight in God, as misers do in gold, and kings in sceptres, you never enjoy the world.

Till your spirit filleth the whole world, and the stars are your jewels; till you are as familiar with the ways of God in all ages as with your walk and table; till you are intimately acquainted with that shady nothing out of which the world was made; till you love men so as to desire their happiness with a thirst equal to the zeal of your own; till you delight in God for being good to all: you never enjoy the world.

Thomas Traherne (c.1636–74), *Centuries of Meditations*

Joined for life

What greater thing is there for two human souls, than to feel they are joined for life – to strengthen each other in all labour, to rest, to rest on each other in all sorrow, to minister to each other in all pain, to be one with each other in silent unspeakable memories.

George Eliot (1819–80), *Adam Bede*

i carry your heart with me

i carry your heart with me(i carry it in
my heart)i am never without it(anywhere
i go you go, my dear; and whatever is done
by only me is your doing, my darling)
                                   i fear
no fate(for you are my fate, my sweet)i want
no world(for beautiful you are my world, my true)
and it's you are whatever a moon has always meant
and whatever a sun will always sing is you

here is the deepest secret nobody knows
(here is the root of the root and the bud of the bud
and the sky of the sky of a tree called life; which grows
higher than soul can hope or mind can hide)
and this is the wonder that's keeping the stars apart

i carry your heart(i carry it in my heart)

E. E. Cummings (1894–1962)

In thanksgiving and joy

Night is drawing nigh –

For all that has been – thanks.
To all that shall be – YES!

Dag Hammarskjöld (1905–61)

Acknowledgements

Where no acknowledgement is made in the anthology, no source or author is known. Every effort has been made to trace copyright ownership of items included in this anthology. The Author and Publishers apologise to those who have not been traced at the time of going to press, and whose rights who have inadvertently not been acknowledged. They would be grateful to be informed of any omissions or inaccuracies in this respect. The Author and Publisher are grateful for permission to reproduce material under copyright, and are grateful to the following copyright holders:

Moncur Street Music Ltd, on behalf of Cherio Corporation, New York, for the lyrics of 'Beware Brother Beware' by Morry Lasco, Dick Adams and Fleecie Moore © 1945, 1946 (Renewed) by Cherio Corp., all rights reserved.

Carlton Publishing Group, on behalf of the Estate of Ogden Nash, for five of his poems, 'To My Valentine', 'The Perfect Husband', 'The Joyous Malingerer', 'I Do, I Will, I Have', and 'A Word To Husbands'.

Darton Longman Todd Ltd, for two extracts from W. H.

Vanstone, *Love's Endeavour, Love's Expense*, London, 1977; and two extracts from Philip Sheldrake, *Befriending our Desires*, 1994.

HarperCollins, for an extract from C. S. Lewis, *Mere Christianity*, 1961.

Rogers, Coleridge and White, 20 Powis Mews, London W11 1JN, acting on behalf of the Estate of Adrian Henri, for his poem 'Love is . . .', from his *Collected Poems,* published by Allison & Busby © Adrian Henri 1987.

W. W. Norton & Co., for E. E. Cummings' poem, 'i carry your heart with me' from his *Complete Poems 1904–1962,* edited by George J. Firmage © 1991 by the Trustees for the E. E. Cummings Trust and George James Firmage.

Index of Biblical Readings

Bible quotations are taken from the *New Revised Standard Version* © 1989 The Division of Christian Education of the National Council of Churches in the USA.

Index of Authors

Index of Titles or First Lines

For each ecstatic instant 68

Gather ye rosebuds while ye may 15
Give me women, wine, and snuff 27

He fumbles at your spirit 15
How can I keep my soul in me 63
How delicious is the winning 76
How do I love thee? Let me count the ways 94

I cannot promise you a life of sunshine 97
I carry your heart with me 100
If ever two were one, then surely we 61
If music be the food of love, play on 22
I love you 50
I love thee 78
I loved thee, though I told thee not 16
I ne'er was struck before that hour 18
In search for intimacy 69
In thanksgiving and joy 101
It is a truth universally acknowledged 34
It was not in winter 4
It was a lover and his lass 3
I wish I could remember 17
I wonder by my troth 47

Jeanie with the light brown hair 9
Joined for life 100

Let me not to the marriage of true minds 54
Love as the giving of self 49

An Invitation to JOIN THE FRIENDS OF

SCM-CANTERBURY PRESS

And save money on your religious book buying ...

Friends of SCM-Canterbury Press is a superb value-for-money membership scheme offering massive savings on both imprints.

BENEFITS OF MEMBERSHIP

- *Exclusive: 20% off all new books published in the year*
- *Exclusive: offers at 50% or more off selected titles from the backlist*
- *Exclusive: offers on Epworth Press and other distributed lists*
- *Exclusive: dedicated website pages, e-mail bulletins, special offers and competitions*

Join now – and start saving money on your book-buying today!

If you would like to join please contact:
The Mailing List Secretary, SCM-Canterbury Press,
9-17 St Albans Place, London N1 0NX
Tel: 00 44(0) 207 359 8034 • Fax: 00 44 (0) 207 359 0049
Email: office@scm-canterburypress.co.uk
PLEASE QUOTE BOOKAD

Alternatively why not join online and gain an extra saving of £2; the members' pages are very easy to use and all online ordering is completely secure.

Join at: www.scm-canterburypress.co.uk
Subscriptions run annually.

2005 Rates: UK £8.00 • International: £10.00